Questions to Ask Yourself Today

In Case Jesus Comes Back Tomorrow

JEANIE PRICE

COPYRIGHT © 1993 BY JEANIE PRICE

All Rights Reserved. First Edition.

No part of this publication may be reproduced, stored in a retrieval system,
or transmitted in any form by any means,
electronic, mechanical, photocopy, recording, or otherwise, without
the prior written permission of the publisher,
except for brief quotations in critical reviews or articles.

Star Song Publishing Group
a division of Jubilee Communications, Inc.
P.O. Box 150009
Nashville, Tennessee 37215

All scripture quotations are from The Holy Bible:
NEW INTERNATIONAL VERSION.
© 1978 by the New York International Bible Society.

ISBN # 1-56233-085-3

Printed in the United States of America
First Printing, September 1993

1 2 3 4 5 6 7 8 9 – 97 96 95 94 93

Questions to Ask Yourself Today

INTRODUCTION

Anyone who has ever attended church camp or a revival or prayer meeting is familiar with the great old hymn "Whisper a Prayer." The third verse is especially powerful:

> *Jesus may come in the morning,*
> *Jesus may come at noon,*
> *Jesus may come in the evening,*
> *So keep your heart in tune.*

Like many of the great songs of the faith, this simple verse is filled with deep spiritual insight. It's true, Jesus is coming again to claim His people. Yet what does this mean? Who are God's people? How do you know if He is pleased with the life that you are living right now—if your heart is truly "in tune"? Is there something you can do to prepare yourself for the coming of the Savior? **Questions to Ask Yourself Today In Case Jesus Comes Back Tomorrow** was written to encourage serious reflection on each of these, and many more, questions. It is also meant to be a lot of fun.

Of course don't forget that each question is for you and you alone. This is your test. You can't answer for yourself while thinking, "Oh yes, this is what so-and-so should be doing." When Jesus does return you will stand alone before Him to be judged. He will not ask you how "so-and-so" should have lived his or her life. Instead He will ask how you conducted yourself according to the standards set forth in His Word. Don't let this fact scare you; instead allow it to challenge you to live a life that will please God. (And, while you're at it, you might as well thank God for "releasing" you from the pressure of being responsible for everyone else's actions.)

Questions to Ask Yourself Today In Case Jesus Comes Back Tomorrow is divided into two parts: *The Book of Questions* and *The Book of Answers*. The former is filled with specific and numbered questions on different aspects of the Christian life. The latter has corresponding numbered "answers" taken directly from Scripture. In other words, while each question is meant to provoke thoughtful and personal responses the reader should know that there is a right and wrong answer that can be found in the Bible.

In addition to personal reflection you will want to read these questions and discuss them in your Sunday school class or study group. This exercise will not only encourage stimulating discussions, it will allow you to be edified by hearing what other people think about the day-to-day challenges of the spirit-filled life as well.

But, most of all, this little book is designed to encourage you to examine your heart and your life. I firmly believe that it is not the big events that make up who and what we are, it is the sum total of all the little seemingly meaningless decisions we make each day that really define us.

The apostle Paul gives us words of instruction: "Examine yourselves to see whether you are in the faith; test yourselves. Do you not realize that Christ Jesus is in you—unless, of course, you fail the test?" (2 Cor. 13:5). So, if you dare, turn the page and begin examining your life in light of God's Word. Do you pass the test?

Your friend in Christ Jesus,

Jeanie Price

JEANIE PRICE
Nashville, Tennessee

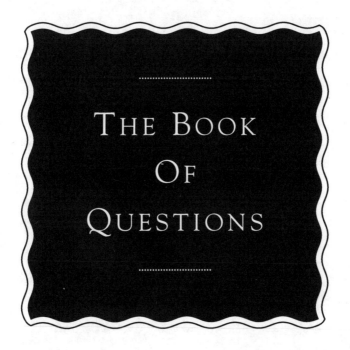

The Book Of Questions

QUESTION 1

What was your reaction the last time a close friend betrayed your confidence? Does it make you angry when your husband, wife, or children leave the cap off of the toothpaste, abandon dirty dishes in the sink, forget to wipe out the tub, or neglect to take care of the car like you do?

QUESTION 2

On matters concerning the opposite sex, do you agree with the popular statement, "You can look but you can't touch?" If you do agree, then list your reasons. When someone of the opposite sex walks past you, do you look them over to see if you find them attractive? What if the person in the office next to your is very attractive (by your definition) and needs to walk past your desk several times throughout the day. Do you look up when they walk by? Does this question make you uncomfortable? Do you ever view pornography?

QUESTION 3

Take a piece of paper and write down everything that you did last Sunday. Did you treat it as though it was a holy day?

QUESTION 4

What tone of voice do you use when speaking to your mother and/or father? What about your in-laws? If your aging parent was no longer able to live alone, what would you do? What if this parent was senile and hostile? Write down fifteen words that accurately describe your mother and/or father. Are these words honorable? If your descriptive words are not honorable do you think that your parents are to blame or do you think that your attitude needs to be redefined?

QUESTION
5

You are driving down the street and, as you approach an intersection, you take your eyes off the road for just a moment to adjust your radio dial. In this instant you are involved in a minor accident with another car. Just the day before you received a notice from your insurance agent stating that if you were involved in another accident that was your fault your insurance payments would double. The police are called and they approach you to find out what happened. You quickly survey the accident scene and find yourself tempted to lead the police to believe that the other driver was at fault. What do you tell them?

QUESTION 6

You are taking a difficult evening class on computer programming. The company that you work for is planning to promote you because of the skills you are acquiring through this course, but only if you pass. The last class is in session and you are sitting at your desk taking the final exam that is worth 75% of your grade. Although you invested a significant amount of time studying, you realize that almost half of the test covers a section of material that you did not fully grasp. Sitting at the table next to you is the class brain—a person who actually knows more about computers than your professor. You can see this person's test paper as clearly as you can see your own. The professor has left the room, and you are absolutely sure that no one is looking. Whose answers do you use to complete your exam?

QUESTION 7

When was the last time you shared your home or a special holiday (Christmas, Thanksgiving, Easter) with someone who does not have a family or for whatever reason might be alone? Do you think you do enough to support people who are alone?

QUESTION 8

Because your Sunday school class has grown out of the small room you were assigned to meet in, you have started gathering around a large table in the fellowship hall. Since the move your class has also been having breakfast together while you meet. One Sunday morning two people approach an empty chair beside you. One of these individuals is very wealthy and generous with the church in their tithes and offerings. The other is supported by public aid, does not have perfect hygiene, and their table manners are abominable. The last time they sat next to you, you could have sworn everyone else thought it was you who forgot to use deodorant. As they both look at each other and then at you to whom do you motion to take the empty seat?

QUESTION 9

You have a hidden sin in your life that no one in your church or family knows about. Although you would like to stop this activity you don't because you receive so much illicit pleasure from it. You have managed to separate this hidden sin from all other aspects of your life. Should you really feel guilty since you know that on Sunday you will go to church, give an extra big offering, and ask God to forgive you?

QUESTION 10

A Christian friend invites you to lunch because they want to talk about a situation in their life. After a few minutes of polite chit-chat your friend becomes serious and shares with you that they are having an affair with someone who is married. Your friend assures you that the person they are involved with is going to get a divorce and that they will then get married. You hesitate for a moment, searching for the right response. As you pause your friend hastily and defensively adds, "Anyone in my situation would do the same thing." What do you say?

QUESTION 11

The paycheck from your full-time job keeps dwindling due to the high rate of inflation and new tax laws. You have taken an additional, part-time job to make ends meet. Although you still can't afford any luxuries, your hard work means that your cupboards are always full of food, you have comfortable clothes to wear, and your home is warm and safe.

• • •

At church one Sunday evening, before the offering plate is passed, the minister announces that a family who attends morning services occasionally is having financial problems. The father has lost his job, the third time this has happened in the past year, and the mother is expecting twins—who will join six other children that the couple have had during their eight years of marriage. They are in desperate need of food, diapers, clothing for the children, and other essentials. This offering is just for them.

• • •

As you listen to your pastor you start thinking about the extra forty dollars in your checking account you have saved so you can go to a concert the following weekend. You have looked forward to this event for quite some time and feel that you deserve to go since you work so hard. As you think about the concert and all of your back-breaking hours on the job you wonder why this man has lost yet another job. And why does this family have so many children if they can't afford to make ends meet? The offering plate is passed to you. What do you do?

QUESTION 12

You have just signed a one-year lease for a charming little house in a quiet neighborhood. The contract doesn't allow you to move unless you pay the rent that would be owed during the remainder of the six month period. Within two weeks of signing the agreement an obnoxious couple buys the house next door. Without any apparent reason they immediately dislike your family and loudly complain about everything from how you mow your lawn to the time of day you turn off your porch light. The new puppy that your children adored is found dead one morning on their front lawn. A friend witnessed the husband scratch the door of your new car in a mall parking lot with his keys. The last straw came when they called the police department and filed a complaint against you for breaking and entering—and the only time you had ever stepped foot on their property was to retrieve the small, limp body of the deceased family pet! You have talked to your landlord but have been informed that you will have to honor the terms of the lease. You can't afford to move and pay for two rental properties. In desperation you drop to your knees and call out to your heavenly Father. How do you pray?

QUESTION 13
....

You and your family have taken a three-day mini-vacation. Everyone has had a great time and you each feel rested and relaxed. As you pull into the driveway, however, something about your house doesn't look quite right. You soon discover that while you were away, someone broke in and stole all of your valuable possessions. You call the police and begin making a list of everything that is missing: jewelry, money you thought was well hidden, silverware, a television set and VCR, the microwave, your children's bicycles, a new set of tools, and much more. You have been thoroughly cleaned out.

. . .

The police investigate, and eventually two eye-witnesses step forward. You are brought into the police station, the police pull a photograph from a manila folder of the suspected thief—someone with a previous record—and you realize that he is a current employee at the business you own. Your blood pressure mounts as you remember the many times you have caught him stealing at work, and the many times he has apologized when you confronted him. You have forgiven him every time and given him another chance; but this time is different. He broke into your home. What if you had returned from your trip a day early and surprised him while he was in your house; would he have killed you? Can you forgive this person yet again?

QUESTION 14

You are serving on the jury of a highly publicized murder trial. Although the media has generally remained neutral and simply reported the facts, most people strongly believe that the defendant in the case is guilty. Yet, after weighing all the evidence, you are firmly convinced that the accused person is innocent. Everyone else on the jury has been swayed by public opinion and has cast their ballot as guilty. If you say that the person is innocent then the result will be a hung jury. You want to do the right thing but you fear for your safety and reputation if people ever find out who cast the deciding ballot. How do you vote?

QUESTION
15

Do you think that a person's nationality or race is important? Do you think that education or social position is important?

QUESTION 16

How often do you respond with horror to the news? Do you worry about the future of America?

QUESTION
17

Each day starts and ends at a hectic and fast pace for you. You have children to care for, breakfast to prepare, dishes to wash, a job that demands all of your creative energy, a boss who requires you to work beyond the typical eight-hour day, a lawn to mow, bills to pay, a car to service and wash, elderly parents to visit, and on and on and on. Do you work so hard that you find yourself exhausted by the many things that claim your time and energy? Do you long for something that you do not have? Is there no rest for you?

QUESTION 18

How much television do you watch in a week? How much time do you spend chatting about nothing in particular over the telephone? How many hours per week do you watch sports? How much time per week do you invest in magazines, books, radio, or movies? How much time each day do you spend eating? After answering these questions do you then find it ironic to say, "I'd love to help out with Vacation Bible School or teach a Sunday school class but I just don't have the time"?

QUESTION 19

How much time each day do you spend in personal hygiene and grooming? Do you spend several hours a week at the mall, browsing through yet another display of sweaters? How many mirrors are in your house? Is your closet too small for your clothes? Do you compare the way you look with the way others look? How much time each day do you spend in prayer and the reading of God's Word?

QUESTION 20

Do you believe that your life would be more content if you were more financially secure?

QUESTION 21

Examine your financial situation honestly. Do you think that your level of integrity is above the kind of evil that is rooted in the love of money?

22

Do you find that many Christians in the public eye are obnoxious or confrontational? Are you ever afraid that other people will associate you with them? When was the last time you presented the message of the gospel to someone? Were you concerned with what that person would think of you for being an active Christian?

QUESTION 23

How often do you say things you wish you had not said? Do you weigh your words carefully or do you speak impulsively? When you are talking to or about another person, are you conscious of the effect your statements will have?

QUESTION 24

Do you think that you cannot like someone and, yet, at the same time, love them through the Lord? Make a list of the people you know that you would lay down your life for; be honest while making this list. Does your list extend beyond your children, spouse, and parents?

QUESTION 25

What do you consider your most valuable possession? Do you spend a lot of time and energy on the possessions that you have? How much time and money do you devote to taking care of your possessions?

QUESTION 26

Your church is in the process of remodeling and you have been elected to head the redecorating committee. The purpose of this committee is to select the color and type of paint to be used, the carpeting, the altar railing, and other details. Everything has been selected and peaceably agreed upon so far except for the carpeting. The committee is split in the middle on the color of carpeting for the sanctuary, and emotions are running high. One group strongly believes the carpet should be blue, the other group strongly feels it should be green.

• • •

You are a respected interior designer and everyone in the church knows that you are the head of this committee. You have put forth an extra effort in making sure each detail, no matter how small, is handled with the utmost taste. The local newspaper has even done an article about the remodeling and has praised your creative genius. You know that whichever color you agree on, the blue or the green, there will be bitterness and hard feelings over the decision. Everyone on the committee has chosen a gray carpeting as their second choice. You know that gray will ruin the balance of color and texture in the sanctuary and you will be a laughingstock among your peers. Yet if you go with gray there will be peace within the church. What color do you choose?

QUESTION 27

Do you think that you should be true to your own way of thinking at all times? What if you are eating in a restaurant with a Christian friend who believes that drinking is wrong. You do not believe that drinking is wrong and you would like to order a glass of wine to go with your meal. Your friend will be bothered if you drink wine. What should you do?

QUESTION 28

Do you feel that your life lacks meaning but you don't know what to do about it? As you get older do the activities that once gave you great pleasure bore you?

QUESTION 29

Does the thought of growing old frighten you or make you feel uneasy? Do you fear being abandoned in your old age?

QUESTION 30

How much attention do you give your family? What if you are tired and have had a long day? Do you find the financial obligation of your children a blessing or a burden?

QUESTION 31

Many people say that you will never love anyone as much as you love your children. If you have children, do you love them more than you love Jesus?

QUESTION 32

You have prayed diligently for something that has been a concern of yours for quite some time. The Lord has not yet answered your prayer and you are becoming impatient. Do you believe that you should stop praying for this concern and put it behind you?

QUESTION 33

Do you think that your life lacks love, joy, peace, patience, kindness, goodness, faithfulness, gentleness, and self-control? Will you allow God to give you these things?

QUESTION 34

Have you ever borrowed money from someone and not paid it back? Do you take seriously any loans you might have with the bank?

QUESTION 35

How do you feel about the current President of the United States? What about the rest of his administration? Do you think that you have done your duty to your country as a Christian by voting and paying your taxes?

QUESTION 36

What do you worry about the most? Your job, other people, your family, money, your health?

QUESTION 37

Do you think that you are better than other people? Do you think that there are people who are better than you?

QUESTION 38

Where does your strength come from?

QUESTION 39

Do you ever curse? How important are the words you say to other people?

QUESTION 40

You have a decision to make that will alter your life and the lives of the people around you. You know what you should do and the people around you are in agreement with you, yet after reading Scripture and bringing this decision before the Lord you believe that God wants you to decide differently. You are reluctant to follow the Lord's guidance because you really do feel that it is not in your best interest. What do you do?

QUESTION 41

There is a difficult situation in your life that you are unable to escape. You do not know if you are strong enough to handle this crisis—yet it doesn't need your "permission" to invade your life. You pray for God to take this situation and resolve it. You look to the people in your church for support and they are unsympathetic. You patiently wait and pray, yet God does not relieve you of your difficulty. Why hasn't God answered your prayer?

QUESTION 42

Your doctor is a member of the church you attend. You have what appears to be a minor ailment and you go to him for diagnosis and treatment. He diagnoses your illness incorrectly, and the treatment that he gives you causes irreparable damage. You will have to live with this serious mistake for the rest of your life. You will not be able to work as much as you could before and you will have to take a different job with less pay because you will be unable to preform your present tasks. You will also have other health problems and will need consistent medical attention for the rest of your life. Should you sue?

QUESTION 43

A Christian friend who attends your church is indulging in a sexual sin. You have counseled and gently reprimanded them for their conduct. Instead of admitting their guilt and seeking God's forgiveness, however, this friend continues to indulge in sexual sin and to rationalize their actions to other people. You are in constant prayer about this but your hands are tied because your friend is not willing to give up their lifestyle or listen to your friendly counsel. One Saturday they call you on the telephone and invite you to have lunch with them after church on Sunday. Do you accept their invitation?

QUESTION 44

The Christian friend referred to in Question 43 was eventually rejected from the fellowship of your church because of their sexual sin. Several years later your friend repents of this sin and returns to your church. How do you respond to them?

QUESTION 45

Do you give regularly to your church or do you withhold your tithe and offerings because you fear you won't have enough money to support yourself? Do you feel pressured to give ten percent of your income? When you put your money in the offering plate do you think about all the things you could do for yourself with that money?

QUESTION 46

Do you ever feel the urge to give up and to quit trying to do what is right?

QUESTION 47

Do you have to tell other people that you are a Christian or do they know this by the way you live your life? Do you ever grieve the Holy Spirit by your actions?

QUESTION 48

How often do you pray?

QUESTION 49

Do you believe that Christians should apply a different code of conduct when involved in a business transaction? Do you believe that Scripture applies to all aspects of your life?

QUESTION 50

Do you ever wonder if you are a Christian?

ANSWER
1

But I tell you that anyone who is angry with his brother will be subject to judgment.

Matthew 5:22

*See also: 2 Corinthians 12:20,
Galatians 5:19-21, Ephesians 4:26, 31,
1 Timothy 2:8, James 1:19*

ANSWER 2

You have heard that it was said, "Do not commit adultery." But I tell you that anyone who looks at a woman lustfully has already committed adultery with her in his heart.

Matthew 5:27-28

See also: Galatians 5:19-21, Hebrews 13:4

ANSWER 3

Remember the Sabbath day by keeping it holy.

Exodus 20:8

*See also: Deuteronomy 5:12-15,
Isaiah 56:2; 58:13-14, Mark 2:27-28*

ANSWER 4

Honor your father and your mother, so that you may live long in the land the LORD your God is giving you.

Exodus 20:12

See also: 1 Timothy 5:8, Titus 1:6

ANSWER
5

Like a club or a sword or a sharp arrow is the man who gives false testimony against his neighbor.

Proverbs 25:18

See also: Proverbs 19:9; 24:28, 1 Timothy 1:10-11

ANSWER 6

He who has been stealing must steal no longer, but must work, doing something useful with his own hands, that he may have something to share with those in need.

Ephesians 4:28

See also: Proverbs 21:6, Isaiah 61:8

ANSWER 7

Religion that God our Father accepts as pure and faultless is this: to look after orphans and widows in their distress and to keep oneself from being polluted by the world.

James 1:27

See also: Deuteronomy 27:19, Matthew 25:35-46

ANSWER 8

If you show special attention to the man wearing fine clothes and say, "Here's a good seat for you," but say to the poor man, "You stand there," or "Sit on the floor by my feet," have you not discriminated among yourselves and become judges with evil thoughts?

James 2:3-4

See also: 1 Timothy 5:21

ANSWER 9

The sacrifice of the wicked is detestable—how much more so when brought with evil intent!

Proverbs 21:27

See also: Psalm 40:6; 50:14, Mark 12:33

ANSWER 10

Brothers, if someone is caught in a sin, you who are spiritual should restore him gently. But watch yourself, or you also may be tempted.

Galatians 6:1

See also: Proverbs 27:5-6; 28:23, Hebrews 3:13

ANSWER 11

He who despises his neighbor sins, but blessed is he who is kind to the needy.

Proverbs 14:21

See also: Psalm 146:5-7, Luke 11:41; 12:33

ANSWER 12

This is how you should pray: "Our Father in heaven, hallowed be your name, your kingdom come, your will be done on earth as it is in heaven. Give us today our daily bread. Forgive us our debts, as we also have forgiven our debtors. And lead us not into temptation, but deliver us from the evil one." For if you forgive men when they sin against you, your heavenly Father will also forgive you.

Matthew 6:9-14

ANSWER 13

Then Peter came to Jesus and asked, "Lord, how many times shall I forgive my brother when he sins against me? Up to seven times?" Jesus answered, "I tell you, not seven times, but seventy-seven times."

Matthew 18:21-22

See also: Mark 11:25, Luke 17:3-4

ANSWER 14

Do not withhold good from those who deserve it, when it is in your power to act.

Proverbs 3:27

See also: Exodus 23:2-3, Zechariah 8:17

ANSWER 15

Here there is no Greek or Jew, circumcised or uncircumcised, barbarian, Scythian, slave or free, but Christ is all, and is in all.

Colossians 3:11

See also: Acts 10:28

ANSWER 16

He changes times and seasons; he sets up kings and deposes them. He gives wisdom to the wise and knowledge to the discerning.

Daniel 2:21

See also: Ecclesiastes 3:11, Jeremiah 32:17

ANSWER 17

Come to me, all you who are weary and burdened, and I will give you rest. Take my yoke upon you and learn from me, for I am gentle and humble in heart, and you will find rest for your souls.

Matthew 11:28-29

See also: Psalm 125:1, Philippians 4:7-9

ANSWER
18

Anyone, then, who knows the good he ought to do and doesn't do it, sins.

James 4:17

See also: Ezekiel 16:49

ANSWER 19

I also want women to dress modestly, with decency and propriety, not with braided hair or gold or pearls or expensive clothes, but with good deeds, appropriate for women who profess to worship God.

1 Timothy 2:9-10

See also: Philippians 2:3-4

ANSWER 20

But godliness with contentment is great gain. For we brought nothing into the world, and we can take nothing out of it. But if we have food and clothing, we will be content with that.

1 Timothy 6:6-8

See also: Hebrews 13:5

ANSWER 21

For the love of money is a root of all kinds of evil. Some people, eager for money, have wandered from the faith and pierced themselves with many griefs.

1 Timothy 6:10

See also: Matthew 6:24-25

ANSWER 22

For God did not give us a spirit of timidity, but a spirit of power, of love and of self-discipline. So do not be ashamed to testify about our Lord, or ashamed of me his prisoner.

2 Timothy 1:7-8

See also: Matthew 28:18-20, Mark 13:10

ANSWER 23

If anyone considers himself religious and yet does not keep a tight rein on his tongue, he deceives himself and his religion is worthless.

James 1:26

See also: Ephesians 4:29, James 3:5

ANSWER 24

This is how we know what love is: Jesus Christ laid down his life for us. And we ought to lay down our lives for our brothers.

1 John 3:16

See also: Luke 6:31-35, 1 Peter 2:1

ANSWER 25

But store up for yourselves treasures in heaven, where moth and rust do not destroy, and where thieves do not break in and steal.

Matthew 6:20

See also: Deuteronomy 8:10-18, Proverbs 15:16

ANSWER 26

I appeal to you, brothers, in the name of our Lord Jesus Christ, that all of you agree with one another so that there may be no divisions among you and that you may be perfectly united in mind and thought.

1 Corinthians 1:10

See also: John 17:21-23, Colossians 3:15

ANSWER 27

Let us therefore make every effort to do what leads to peace and to mutual edification. Do not destroy the work of God for the sake of food. All food is clean, but it is wrong for a man to eat anything that causes someone else to stumble.

Romans 14:19-20

See also: Romans 14:17, 1 Corinthians 10:28-32

ANSWER 28

However, I consider my life worth nothing to me, if only I may finish the race and complete the task the Lord Jesus has given me—the task of testifying to the gospel of God's grace.

Acts 20:24

See also: Ecclesiastes 12:13, John 10:10

ANSWER 29

Even to your old age and gray hairs I am he, I am he who will sustain you. I have made you and I will carry you; I will sustain you and I will rescue you.

Isaiah 46:4

See also: Psalm 92:14, Proverbs 16:31

ANSWER 30

If anyone does not provide for his relatives, and especially for his immediate family, he has denied the faith and is worse than an unbeliever.

1 Timothy 5:8

See also: 1 Timothy 3:4-5, 1 Timothy 5:4

ANSWER 31

Anyone who loves his father or mother more than me is not worthy of me; anyone who loves his son or daughter more than me is not worthy of me; and anyone who does not take his cross and follow me is not worthy of me.

Matthew 10:37-38

ANSWER 32

But if we hope for what we do not yet have, we wait for it patiently.

Romans 8:25

See also: Psalm 116:2, Romans 12:12, Colossians 4:2

ANSWER 33

But the fruit of the Spirit is love, joy, peace, patience, kindness, goodness, faithfulness, gentleness and self-control. Against such things there is no law. Those who belong to Christ Jesus have crucified the sinful nature with its passions and desires.

Galatians 5:22-24

ANSWER
3 4

The wicked borrow and do not repay, but the righteous give generously. They are always generous and lend freely; their children will be blessed.

Psalm 37:21, 26

See also: Romans 13:8

ANSWER 35

I urge, then, first of all, that requests, prayers, intercession and thanksgiving be made for everyone—for kings and all those in authority, that we may live peaceful and quiet lives in all godliness and holiness.

1 Timothy 2:1-2

ANSWER 36

Do not be anxious about anything, but in everything, by prayer and petition, with thanksgiving, present your requests to God.

Philippians 4:6

ANSWER 37

Do nothing out of selfish ambition or vain conceit, but in humility consider others better than yourselves.

Philippians 2:3

See also: Romans 12:3, 1 Corinthians 3:18

ANSWER 38

Finally, be strong in the Lord and in his mighty power.

Ephesians 6:10

See also: Isaiah 40:29-31

ANSWER 39

Do not let any unwholesome talk come out of your mouths, but only what is helpful for building others up according to their needs, that it may benefit those who listen.

Ephesians 4:29

See also: Proverbs 13:3, Matthew 12:36-37, Ephesians 5:4

ANSWER 40

Trust in the L ORD with all your heart and lean not on your own understanding; in all your ways acknowledge him, and he will make your paths straight.

Proverbs 3:5-6

See also: Proverbs 3:7, Colossians 2:8, James 1:5-8

ANSWER 41

Three times I pleaded with the Lord to take it away from me. But he said to me, "My grace is sufficient for you, for my power is made perfect in weakness." Therefore I will boast all the more gladly about my weaknesses, so that Christ's power may rest on me.

2 Corinthians 12:8-9

See also: Revelation 14:12

ANSWER 42

If any of you has a dispute with another, dare he take it before the ungodly for judgment instead of before the saints? Do you not know that the saints will judge the world? And if you are to judge the world, are you not competent to judge trivial cases? Do you not know that we will judge angels? How much more the things of this life! Therefore, if you have disputes about such matters, appoint as judges even men of little account in the church!

1 Corinthians 6:1-4

ANSWER 43

I have written you in my letter not to associate with sexually immoral people—not at all meaning the people of this world who are immoral, or the greedy and swindlers, or idolaters. In that case you would have to leave this world. But now I am writing you that you must not associate with anyone who calls himself a brother but is sexually immoral or greedy, an idolater or a slanderer, a drunkard or a swindler. With such a man do not even eat.

1 Corinthians 5:9-11

ANSWER
44

The punishment inflicted on him by the majority is sufficient for him. Now instead, you ought to forgive and comfort him, so that he will not be overwhelmed by excessive sorrow. I urge you, therefore, to reaffirm your love for him.

2 Corinthians 2:6-8

ANSWER
45

Each man should give what he has decided in his heart to give, not reluctantly or under compulsion, for God loves a cheerful giver. And God is able to make all grace abound to you, so that in all things at all times, having all that you need, you will abound in every good work.

2 Corinthians 9:7-8

See also: 1 Corinthians 16:2, 2 Corinthians 8:11-14

ANSWER 46

Let us not become weary in doing good, for at the proper time we will reap a harvest if we do not give up.

Galatians 6:9

See also: Hebrews 12:1-5, 2 Timothy 3:14

ANSWER 47

And do not grieve the Holy Spirit of God, with whom you were sealed for the day of redemption. Get rid of all bitterness, rage and anger, brawling and slander, along with every form of malice. Be kind and compassionate to one another, forgiving each other, just as in Christ God forgave you. Be imitators of God, therefore, as dearly loved children and live a life of love, just as Christ loved us and gave himself up for us as a fragrant offering and sacrifice to God.

Ephesians 4:30-32; 5:1-2

ANSWER 48

And pray in the Spirit on all occasions with all kinds of prayers and requests. With this in mind, be alert and always keep on praying for all the saints.

Ephesians 6:18

See also: 1 Thessalonians 5:17

ANSWER 49

Now this is our boast: Our conscience testifies that we have conducted ourselves in the world, and especially in our relations with you, in the holiness and sincerity that are from God. We have done so not according to worldly wisdom but according to God's grace.

2 Corinthians 1:12

See also: Galatians 5:25

ANSWER 50

He is the atoning sacrifice for our sins, and not only for ours but also for the sins of the whole world. We know that we have come to know him if we obey his commands. The man who says, "I know him," but does not do what he commands is a liar, and the truth is not in him. But if anyone obeys his word, God's love is truly made complete in him. This is how we know we are in him: Whoever claims to live in him must walk as Jesus did.

1 John 2:2-6